The Restless Sea

SHIFTING SHORES

CAROLE GARBUNY VOGEL

Franklin Watts

A Division of Scholastic Inc.
New York • Toronto • London • Auckland • Sydney
Mexico City • New Delhi • Hong Kong
Danbury, Connecticut

TO RICHIE, NATHANIEL, AND MICAH BARSHAY

Acknowledgments

Many thanks to Professor Peter Guth, Oceanography Department, U.S. Naval Academy, who took time from his busy schedule to read and critique the manuscript and answer my many questions. His vast knowledge of the field and keen insight were reflected in his comments.

I am indebted to Kathleen Derzipilski, a San Diego–based editorial researcher, for her extremely thorough job of fact checking.

I am also grateful to fellow writer Dr. Joyce A. Nettleton for her invaluable criticism, scientific expertise, and sense of humor. Special thanks to students Stephen, Daniel, and Joanna Guth for reading the manuscript from the kid perspective.

As usual, I am indebted to the reference librarians at Cary Memorial Library in Lexington, Massachusetts, for their invaluable assistance in tracking down hard-to-find information.

My sincere appreciation to my husband, Mark A. Vogel, for the encouragement and understanding that has become his hallmark. I would also like to acknowledge the many other people who helped either directly or indirectly.

Finally, my heartfelt thanks to my editor, Kate Nunn, for having faith in my writing ability and the talent to turn my manuscripts into spectacular books.

Photographs © 2003: Corbis Images: 36, 37, 50 (AFP), 39 (Yann Arthus-bertrand), 20 (Bettman), 32 (Gary Braasch), 8 (Sergio Dorantes), 67 (Aaron Horowitz), 54, 55 (William Manning), 23 (Werner H. Muller), 43 (Douglas Peebles), 26, 27 (Roger Ressmeyer), 7, 60, 61 (Reuters NewMedia Inc.), 57 (Lynda Richardson), 28 (Bill Ross), 34, 35 (Galen Rowell), cover (Richard Hamilton Smith), 40 (James A. Sugar), 16, 17 (Mike Waggoner), 53; Getty Images/Benjamin Shearn/Taxi: 12; Photo Researchers, NY/SPL: 63 (Julian Baum), 9 (Lynette Cook), 4 (David Hardy), 25 (Los Alamos National Laboratory), 64, 65 (Claus Lunau/Bonnier Publications), 68, 69 (Novosti Press Agency), 67 inset (Detlev Van Ravenswaay), 71 (Erik Viktor); Stone/Getty Images/James Randklev: 47; The Image Bank/Getty Images: 58 (Theo Allofs), 1 (Ed Freeman).

Illustrations by Al Lorenz
Book design by Marie O'Neill

Library of Congress Cataloging-in-Publication Data

Vogel, Carole Garbuny.
  Shifting shores / by Carole G. Vogel.
    p. cm. — (The restless sea)
Summary: Looks beneath the ocean's surface at the shifting of tectonic plates, the relationship between ocean and climate, and the complex paths of currents that thread the seas.
Includes bibliographical references and index.
  ISBN 0-531-12322-7
  1. Tsunamis—Juvenile literature. 2. Plate tectonics—Juvenile literature. 3. Natural disasters—Juvenile literature. [1. Tsunamis. 2. Plate tectonics. 3. Natural disasters.] I. Title.
  GC221.5.V64 2003
  551.46—dc21
                                    2003005305

contents

chapter 1

TSUNAMIS

Along the north coast of Papua New Guinea lies a narrow spit of land, fringed with palm trees and fishing villages. One side faces the open ocean. The other borders a lagoon that separates the sandy strip from the mainland. At twilight on July 17, 1998, a loud boom shattered the tranquillity of this tropical expanse. An earthquake jolted the ground and long cracks opened in the sand.

Many of the villagers who made their home on this spit rushed onto the beach to see what was going on. As they gathered, the ocean pulled back from the shore, leaving the seafloor bare. Five minutes of silence followed, and then the people heard a rumble like an approaching jet. The rumble grew into a thunderous roar as a tsunami—a mountain of water—barreled toward shore.

The people tried to run away, but the wave overtook them. Two more monster waves followed. The largest rose to the height of a four-story building. The waves flattened four villages and killed about 3,000 people. More than 550 survivors suffered critical injures when the waves slammed them against trees and other objects. Nearly 5,000 people lost their homes.

Initially scientists thought that an earthquake had generated the tsunami by lifting the seafloor. Movement of the ocean bottom is the most common cause of tsunamis. When the seafloor rises or falls, it moves the entire mountain of water on top of it—all the way from the ocean bottom to the surface.

The effect is similar to what happens when you thunk the outside of a small plastic wading pool. The moving plastic pushes water out of the way. The displaced water has to go somewhere. In a wading pool, it produces a large wave that may spill over the top.

In the ocean, displaced water turns into tsunami waves. Rising only a foot (30 centimeters) or so above normal wave height, the waves spread out in all directions and race across the ocean. As they near a shallow coastline, the waves begin

Tsunamis pose a deadly threat to communities along the coast of Japan and other nations bordering the Pacific Ocean.

to grow. The water may loom into a towering wall of water, a series of breaking waves, or a fast-rising tide.

Movement of the seafloor did not alone cause the Papua New Guinea tsunami. To be powerful enough to produce a tsunami, earthquakes generally need a moment magnitude of at least 7.5. The moment-magnitude scale rates earthquakes by calculating the total amount of energy they release. This quake, with a magnitude of 7.1, missed the mark. However it set off a giant underwater landslide. The avalanche of mud and sand pushed aside the seawater in its path. This displaced water triggered a local tsunami that battered a relatively small section of the nearby coastline—a 12-mile (19-kilometer) stretch. But the tsunami lacked the energy to cross the ocean and produce large waves at distant sites.

It was a different story, however, on April 1, 1946. A major earthquake off of Alaska's Aleutian Islands set a tsunami in motion that killed people and destroyed property along Alaskan waters and on distant shores. Within 20 minutes of the temblor, a 115-foot (35-meter) wave swept away a lighthouse on Unimak Island, 95 miles (153 kilometers) from the quake's origin. Five men perished.

Tsunami waves sped across the Pacific Ocean. Five hours and 2,300 miles (3,700 kilometers) later the waves walloped the city of Hilo on the Big Island of Hawaii, killing 96 people. A few other communities on the Big Island suffered catastrophic damage, too. But most communities escaped serious harm. The shape of the coast and the direction from which a tsunami appears determine its destructive potential.

VOLCANOES AND TSUNAMIS

Active volcanoes can mean tsunami trouble, too. In May 1883, Krakatau—a tiny volcanic island in Indonesia—roared to life, ending a 200-year silence. Ash and steam streamed out from a central crater. Lightning danced in the blast cloud and jumped between land and sky. Within a week, the eruptions slackened. Still, the inhabitants of the nearby islands of Sebesi, Java, and Sumatra watched the volcano with growing unease.

In 1992 a tsunami swept tuna onto the streets of Maumere on the island of Flores near Portugal. The destructive wave killed more than 2,000 people.

An ash cloud rolls into the atmosphere from the Krakatau volcano during a 1995 eruption. The volcano is gradually rebuilding itself since the cataclysmic explosion of 1883.

At one o'clock on the afternoon of August 26, 1883, their worst fears were realized. A deafening blast rocked the island. Explosion followed explosion as steam and ash billowed from Krakatau's crater. Within one hour, a cloud 17 miles (27 kilometers) high blackened the sky, hiding the island from view. Into the evening and throughout the night, Krakatau pelted out ash and large chunks of volcanic rock. The tumult generated several sets of small tsunamis that ranged from 3 to 6 feet (1 to 2 meters) high when they struck neighboring islands. Early the next morning, a more ominous 33-foot (10-meter) tsunami arose.

Around 10:00 A.M., an eerie silence descended. It appeared as if the volcano were spent. However everything that had occurred up to that point had been only an awesome prelude. A few minutes later, the island of Krakatau blew apart in one of the most violent explosions in history. A column of hot gases and ash shot 25 miles (40 kilometers) high into the atmosphere. The blast pulverized two-thirds of the island. Immense pyroclastic flows—glowing clouds of hot gas and debris—rampaged down the volcano's flanks. Where the summit had been, a caldera—a vast pit 4 miles (6 kilometers) across and 980 feet (300 meters) deep—appeared.

This is how one artist imagined the giant tsunami created by Krakatau's violent eruption.

As a result of the cataclysm, a tsunami zoomed outward from the island in a huge widening circle. Within minutes it approached Sebesi, Java, and Sumatra. The wave grew higher as the seabed became shallower. By the time it slammed onto shore, the tsunami was a lethal wall of water more than 115 feet (35 meters) high. The wave thundered over 300 coastal villages in the region, traveling up to 10 miles (16 kilometers) inland. The villagers could not outrun the tsunami. The water swept away people and crushed buildings. More giant waves followed. The death toll from Krakatau's eruption surpassed 36,000. Most of the causalities resulted from the tsunamis.

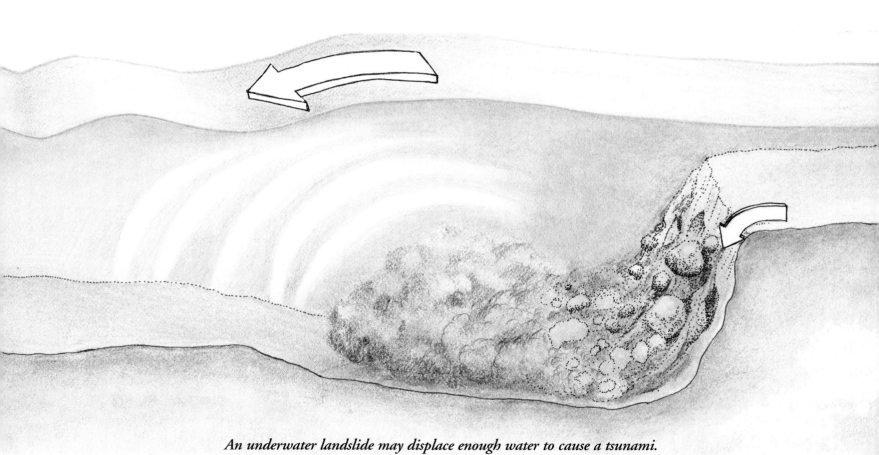

An underwater landslide may displace enough water to cause a tsunami.

Geologists have two likely explanations for the formation of these killer waves. One theory suggests that pyroclastic flows produced them. According to this account, the heavier parts of the flow plunged down the volcano's slopes all the way to the sea bottom. Like a gargantuan undersea landslide, the flow displaced water.

The other theory suggests that an underwater explosion cracked the side of the volcano. Cold seawater rushed in and came in contact with the superhot molten rock inside the volcano. The water flashed to steam and blew the island apart. The force of this megablast produced the monster tsunami. Perhaps both processes were at work during Krakatau's death throes.

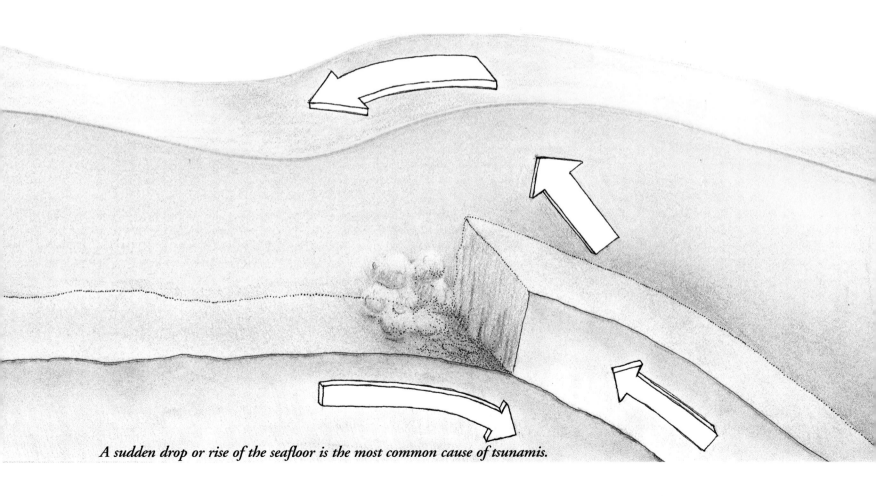

A sudden drop or rise of the seafloor is the most common cause of tsunamis.

If you toss a stone into a pond, the stone displaces the water. After the initial splash, raised ripples of water spread away in a circular pattern from where the stone plunked down. The ripples are waves. Tsunami waves rush away from their starting point in the same way.

Tsunami Waves

Wind creates most ocean waves. Wind blows over the water, dragging the water surface with it, making waves. In the process, wind energy is transferred to the water. The more energy in a wave, the farther it can move. As a wave travels, it carries energy from one place to another.

Like a wind-generated wave, a tsunami wave has a crest (the high point) and a trough (the low point). The distance between the crest and the trough is the wave height. The wavelength is the distance between crests. The time it takes for two crests to pass a specific point is called the period.

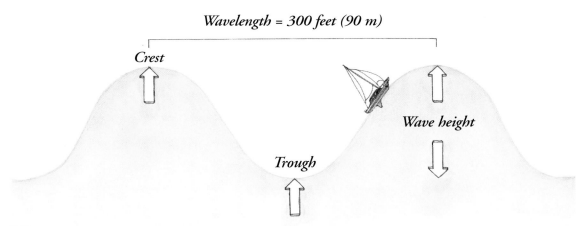

Wavelength = 300 feet (90 m)

Crest

Wave height

Trough

WIND-GENERATED WAVE IN THE OPEN OCEAN

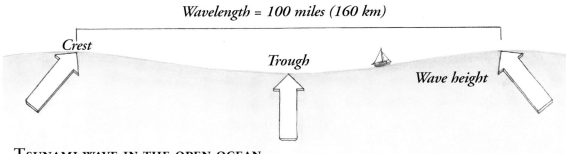

Wavelength = 100 miles (160 km)

Crest

Trough

Wave height

TSUNAMI WAVE IN THE OPEN OCEAN

Tsunamis have extremely long wavelengths. The distance between two tsunami crests may exceed 100 miles (160 kilometers). As a result, tsunami waves have remarkably long periods, ranging from 10 minutes to 2 hours. Wind-driven waves have scrawnier wavelengths, about 100 to 2,000 feet (30 to 600 meters). Most have periods of only 5 to 20 seconds.

Powerful storm winds can generate waves 36 feet (11 meters) high. Their wavelengths are much shorter than the wavelengths of tsunami waves. In a raft, you could zip from the top of a storm wave to its bottom in 7 seconds.

If a tsunami wave rolled under you in the open ocean, you wouldn't notice it. Far from land, the height of a tsunami wave is about a foot (30 centimeters). In addition the wavelength is so long that it would take you 5 to 60 minutes to pass from the top of the wave to the bottom.

Water Particles in Orbit

When wind-driven waves ruffle the ocean surface, the water itself does not travel. The energy of the wave spins the water particles in a circle, or orbit. The particles whiz forward, downward, and then back to their original positions. Beneath the surface, the particles rotate, too. However as the water gets deeper, the orbits get smaller. Finally at a depth equal to one-half the wavelength, the movement dies out completely. Wind-driven waves rarely disturb the water below a depth of 500 feet (150 meters).

When a tsunami travels across the ocean, it forces water particles to move in ellipses—long flattened circles. The particles glide forward about 65 feet (20 meters) or so and then loop back to where they started. Because their wavelengths are so long, tsunami waves affect water particles from the surface all the way to the seafloor—even when tsunamis pass over deep-sea trenches.

In 1896 an earthquake off the Sanriku coast of Japan sent tsunami waves surging out in all directions. Fifteen miles (24 meters) from shore, the waves slipped undetected beneath the boats of local fishermen. When the fishermen returned home, they were stunned by the horror that met them. Floating in the water were the battered hulks of houses, the lifeless bodies of family and friends, and the occasional survivor clinging to wreckage. More than 28,000 people had

Particle movement in a wind-driven wave

No wave motion

Particle movement in a tsunami wave

died when waves as high as 125 feet (38 meters) had crashed down on the unprepared villagers.

The energy of tsunami waves is not concentrated near the ocean surface like the energy of wind-driven waves. It is spread over an enormous region, from the surface down to the seafloor, for the entire length of the wave. (Remember the wavelength of just one tsunami wave can exceed 100 miles!)

Wind-driven waves usually travel across the ocean at speeds familiar to people who ride in cars—15 to 70 miles (24 to 113 kilometers) per hour. But tsunamis can attain speeds that rival jetliners—more than 600 miles (960 kilometers) per hour. The greater the depth, the faster a tsunami wave moves.

As a tsunami approaches shallower water near shore, a transformation occurs. The wave bottom drags along the seafloor and slows. The wavelength shortens, compressing the energy of the wave into a smaller area of water. As a result, the height of the wave increases, piling up water. As the waves grow taller, they bunch up.

Most ocean waves are wind-driven.

If the trough of a tsunami hits the shore first, the wave acts like a giant vacuum cleaner and sucks the water away from the seabed. As the water retreats, the newly exposed seafloor may be strewn with flopping fish, beautiful seashells, and beached boats. If you ever see such a sight, run for your life. When the crest reaches the shore, it will bring a drastic rise in sea level.

THE TSUNAMI WARNING SYSTEM

To reduce the death toll from tsunamis in the Pacific, experts devised the Tsunami Warning System. Earthquakes and water heights are monitored at stations around the Pacific. A tsunami warning is given when an earthquake of

A tsunami coming ashore. The wave height of a tsunami is so low over the ocean the wave passes unnoticed. But near shore, the wave height increases dramatically.

Ocean floor

Earthquake

6.75 magnitude or greater occurs in the Pacific Ocean or along its borders and unusual changes in sea levels are detected.

Because tsunamis are so unpredictable, the system has not been perfected yet. False alarms are a frustrating problem. In addition local tsunamis can reach the shore within minutes of formation, leaving little time for a warning to be issued. No tsunami warning system exists for the Atlantic coast. But the risk of tsunamis there is much less than for the communities along the Pacific Rim or on the coastlines of Pacific islands. If you are by the ocean anywhere, move to higher ground immediately if you:

• feel the ground rumble or shake,
• notice a rapid rise or fall in the sea level,
• hear a loud roar coming from the ocean, or
• hear a tsunami warning.

Keep away from rivers or streams that lead to the ocean since tsunamis can roll up them. Stay on higher ground until local authorities announce that the danger has passed. Tsunamis usually travel in a series and the first wave may be the smallest. Don't assume the danger is over if one or two waves have struck. The time lapse between waves can be more than 30 minutes. As many as eight hours may pass between the first and last waves. Awareness of tsunami warning signs should be part of the education of every child who lives near the ocean or visits one.

chapter 2

A GLIMPSE INSIDE THE EARTH

On the afternoon of Good Friday, March 27, 1964, a tremendous earthquake rocked the coast around Anchorage, Alaska. For four agonizing minutes the land bucked up and down. Humongous gashes split open the streets of Anchorage. Buildings and bridges collapsed. Numerous landslides and avalanches roared down steep hills and mountainsides, stripping them of vegetation and sometimes houses. The quake killed 131 people. Most of them died in monster sea waves set in motion by the quake.

The earthquake lifted the Alaskan coastline by 33 feet (9 meters) in some places and dropped it by as much as 8 feet (2.4 meters) in others. Where the land rose, it destroyed the usefulness of harbors by leaving wharves high and dry. Fishing boats could no longer pull alongside the docks.

Where the land sank, the sea rushed in. Pine forests once above the ocean's reach drowned in seawater. Some seaside villages experienced flooding with the highest tides, forcing residents to abandon their homes.

The Alaskan earthquake measured 9.2 on the moment-magnitude scale, making it the second-most powerful earthquake ever recorded. The most powerful one, a 9.5-magnitude quake, ravaged Chile in 1960. It lifted sections of the Andes Mountains as much as 20 feet (6 meters). Earthquakes ranked below 5.0 on the moment-magnitude scale create little damage. Earthquakes ranked above 5.0 can cause massive destruction.

INSIDE THE EARTH

Thousands of earthquakes occur daily on the planet but most cannot be felt. Geologists estimate that about 900 temblors each year have the strength to destroy buildings and snuff out lives. Fortunately most of the damaging quakes strike remote regions with few people.

This street in Anchorage, Alaska, dropped 20 feet (6 m) during the 1964 Good Friday earthquake.

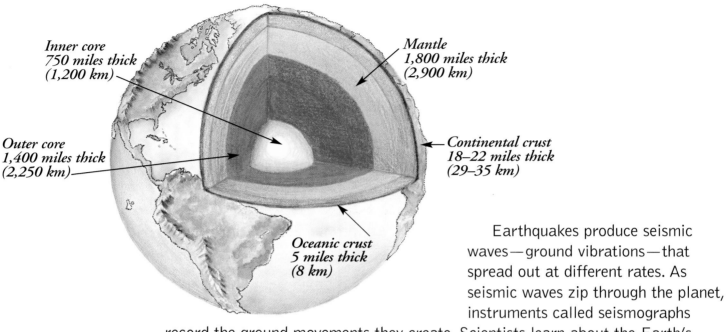

Inner core
750 miles thick
(1,200 km)

Mantle
1,800 miles thick
(2,900 km)

Outer core
1,400 miles thick
(2,250 km)

Continental crust
18–22 miles thick
(29–35 km)

Oceanic crust
5 miles thick
(8 km)

Earthquakes produce seismic waves—ground vibrations—that spread out at different rates. As seismic waves zip through the planet, instruments called seismographs record the ground movements they create. Scientists learn about the Earth's inner structure by comparing the speed of different seismic waves and their paths. Like X rays providing an image of the human skeleton, seismic waves produce a picture of the Earth's insides.

From seismic-wave data, geologists determined that the Earth's interior consists of four major layers—the crust, mantle, outer core, and inner core. If you could tunnel through these layers to the center of the Earth, the deeper you journeyed the hotter the surrounding rock would become. The heat arises partly from the decay of radioactive elements within the Earth and partly from the heat left over from the birth of the planet. The innermost layer, the inner core, may be as hot as the surface of the sun.

A mix of heavy metals—mainly iron and some nickel—forms the inner core. The extreme pressure created by the layers above squeezes the inner core so tightly it remains a solid. It cannot expand and become liquid. About one-third the size of the Moon, the inner core is a freely spinning, gigantic metal ball inside the Earth. It rotates more quickly than the rest of the planet.

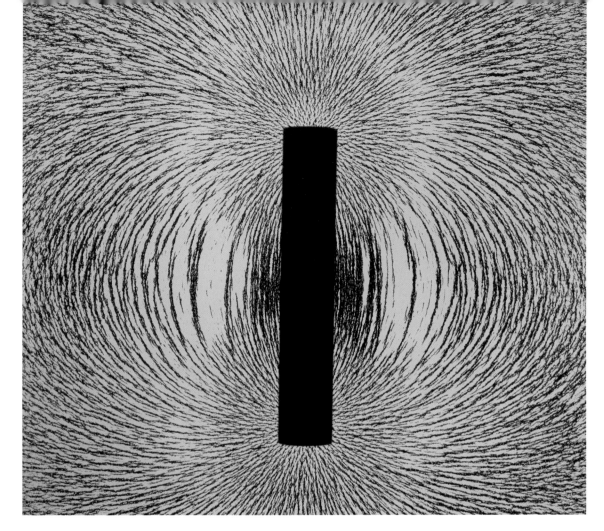

A magnetic field is the area around a magnet where its force attracts objects. A bar magnet attracts iron filings most strongly at its poles.

Wrapped around the inner core is a seething sea of molten metal called the outer core. Like the inner core, the outer core consists of iron and nickel. The outer core acts like a liquid. Swirling currents in the outer core make the inner core spin. Together, the inner and outer cores produce the Earth's magnetic field.

This magnetic field turns the whole planet into a huge bar magnet. The force is strongest at the magnetic poles, which lie near the geographic North and South poles. You can observe the effects of the Earth's magnetic field with a compass. The compass needle's north-seeking end will turn toward the Earth's magnetic north.

Cloaking the outer core is the mantle, a thick layer of hot rock, rich in silicon, oxygen, iron, and magnesium. The boundary between the outer core and mantle is not a smooth one. Upside-down mountains cling to the base of the mantle like stalactites hanging from the top of a cave. Currents of molten metal from the outer core flow across this rugged landscape in the same way winds sweep over mountain peaks at the surface.

The mantle extends from the outer core to just below the surface of the Earth. The mantle consists of three sublayers of rock. The bottom layer is hotter and under greater pressure than the rest of the mantle. As a result, its particles are packed closely together and form a solid mass.

The rock in the middle mantle is less rigid. Like warm, soft candle wax, this rock can bend. It forms a slow-moving layer called the asthenosphere. (*Asthenes* is the Greek word for "weak.")

The upper mantle is colder than the asthenosphere and consists mainly of hard rock. Together with the overlying crust, it creates the solid lithosphere. (*Lithos* is the Greek word for "stone.") Like icebergs floating on the ocean, the lithosphere floats atop the asthenosphere.

The lithosphere is broken into large slabs called tectonic plates. The plates fit snugly together like the parts of a jigsaw puzzle. Riding piggyback atop the plates are the continents and the ocean floor. The plates form the Earth's thin and brittle outer surface, the crust. The crust is thinnest below the oceans, where it averages a mere 5 miles (8 kilometers) in depth. The typical thickness of continental crust, the crust below the continents, ranges from 18 to 22 miles (29 to 35 kilometers). However underneath towering mountains, continental crust may reach a depth as great as 47 miles (76 kilometers). Many plates carry both oceanic and continental crust. For example, the North American plate, which transports most of North America, also carries a large segment of the Atlantic Ocean floor.

CONVECTION CURRENTS: ALL STIRRED UP

Our planet leaks heat. Through convection currents, the Earth transfers heat from its blistering interior to the cooler lithosphere. You can observe convection when you prepare cocoa on a stove. The cocoa at the bottom of the pot becomes hot

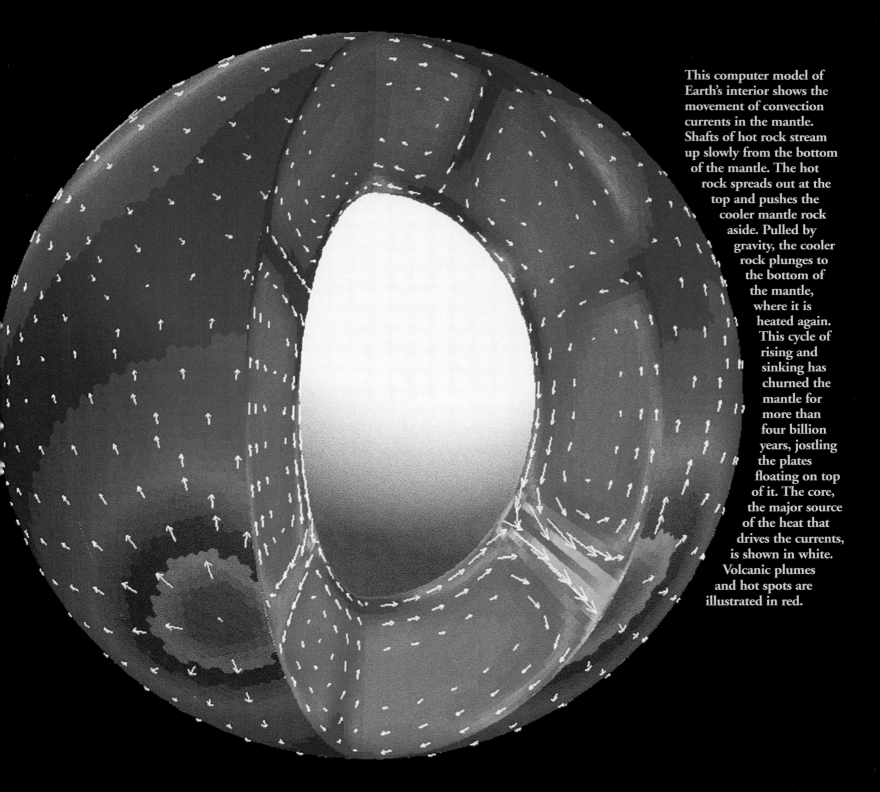

This computer model of Earth's interior shows the movement of convection currents in the mantle. Shafts of hot rock stream up slowly from the bottom of the mantle. The hot rock spreads out at the top and pushes the cooler mantle rock aside. Pulled by gravity, the cooler rock plunges to the bottom of the mantle, where it is heated again. This cycle of rising and sinking has churned the mantle for more than four billion years, jostling the plates floating on top of it. The core, the major source of the heat that drives the currents, is shown in white. Volcanic plumes and hot spots are illustrated in red.

and rises to the surface. As the hot cocoa rises, it nudges the cold cocoa at the top out of the way. The cold cocoa sinks to the bottom, where it is in turn heated.

Convection is the movement of heat in a fluid or gas from a warm place to a cooler one. As the particles of cocoa are heated at the bottom of the pot, they move faster and spread apart. When the particles spread apart, they take up more space and their density decreases. (Density is the amount of mass in a given volume.)

Warm cocoa is less dense than the cooler cocoa around it. So the warm cocoa rises, carrying heat energy with it. A steady circular flow—a convection current—begins as cooler, denser cocoa drops down and replaces the warmer cocoa. The convection currents distribute the heat throughout the cocoa. They also move the marshmallows floating on the surface. The marshmallows crash, pull apart, and glide past each other, all at the whim of the currents.

Fueled by heat from the Earth's core and mantle, convection currents within the mantle drive the tectonic plates in a similar manner. As the plates move, they collide, rip apart, or scrunch past one another. These movements give rise to some of the Earth's most spectacular surface features—volcanoes, mountain ranges, rift valleys, and deep-sea trenches. They also unleash some of the world's cruelest disasters—deadly earthquakes, tsunamis, and volcanic eruptions.

A cave-in permits a glimpse of molten lava flowing in a lava tube just below the surface of Kilauea volcano, Hawaii.

26

chapter 3

THE UPS AND DOWNS OF PLATE MOVEMENTS

Seattle is nestled next to Puget Sound in Washington State, about 90 miles (145 kilometers) from the Pacific Ocean. Surrounded by lakes, rivers, and mountains, the Seattle area is home to Starbucks, Microsoft, the Mariners baseball team, and 3 1/2 million people. The city basks in the shadow of snowcapped Mount Rainier, the highest volcano in the Cascade Range.

A collision between the North American continent and a small oceanic plate off the Pacific Northwest has created an active fault zone that runs beneath Seattle. About three hundred years ago a magnitude-9 earthquake struck the area, and three magnitude-7 quakes shook the region during the twentieth century. It is only a matter of time before the next Big One hits the city.

In 2001, residents got a taste of things to come when the Nisqually earthquake, a 6.8-magnitude temblor, jolted the region. This quake was slightly stronger than the 6.7-magnitude Northridge earthquake that shook Los Angeles, California, in 1994, killing 57 people and causing widespread destruction. Only one person died during the Nisqually earthquake—a victim of a heart attack. And the only large building to sustain major structural damage was the state capitol building in Olympia. The residents of the Puget Sound region were lucky this time. The difference between the quakes was the depth at which they started. The focus, or origin, of the Northridge temblor was 11 miles (18 kilometers) beneath the surface. The Nisqually quake focus was much deeper—33 miles (53 kilometers) down.

SLAMMING PLATES (CONVERGENT BOUNDARIES)

Faults—cracks in the crust where rocks have scraped past each other—mark the boundaries between plates. Three different kinds of boundaries exist: convergent, transform, and divergent. Earthquakes are common along all of them.

Beautiful Mount Rainier in Washington state could turn deadly if a huge landslide or major earthquake set a mudflow in motion.

MAJOR TECTONIC PLATES

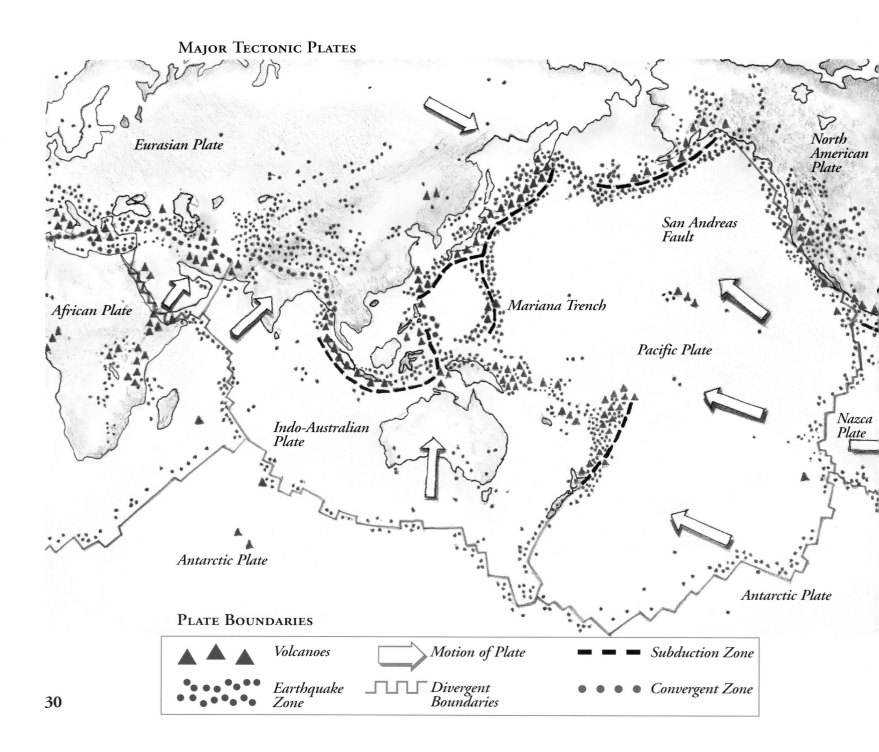

Eurasian Plate

North American Plate

African Plate

San Andreas Fault

Mariana Trench

Pacific Plate

Indo-Australian Plate

Nazca Plate

Antarctic Plate

Antarctic Plate

PLATE BOUNDARIES

▲ ▲ ▲ Volcanoes

● ● ● ● Earthquake Zone

⇨ Motion of Plate

⌐⌐ Divergent Boundaries

▬ ▬ ▬ Subduction Zone

● ● ● ● Convergent Zone

Continental-Oceanic Collisions. Where plates slam together, convergent boundaries form and earthquakes, volcanoes, and mountains result. Density rules here. The density of oceanic crust is much greater than that of continental crust. So when a plate hauling the ocean floor smashes into a plate lugging a continent, the denser oceanic plate plunges beneath the less dense continental plate. This is like oil and vinegar forming separate layers in a salad dressing, only on a titanic scale.

In a process known as subduction, a deep-sea trench (a canyon), develops as the ocean floor bends downward. Dragged by gravity, the ocean floor slips underneath the continent into the asthenosphere. However it is not an easy ride. The jagged edges of the plates snag and build up stress. When the plates finally lurch past each other, they can set off a gargantuan earthquake. This type of movement triggered Alaska's Good Friday earthquake and threatens Seattle. It also fuels volcanoes.

In the Pacific Northwest the subduction process supplies magma to Mount Rainier, Mount St. Helens, and the other Cascade volcanoes. As the descending oceanic plate sinks into the hot asthenosphere, it begins to "sweat." It releases water vapor and other gases that it held in its rocks. Extremely hot, the freed "sweat" seeps up into the overriding continental plate, where it melts the rock. The molten rock—called magma—is less dense

The May 18, 1980, eruption of Mount St. Helens alerted residents of Oregon and Washington to the destructive potential of the Cascade volcanoes.

than the surrounding rock. It oozes upward through cracks in the plate.

Usually the magma collects below the surface, slowly lifting the land overhead and forming the backbone of lofty mountains, such as the Sierra Nevadas in California and Nevada. But occasionally the magma bursts through the surface and spawns a chain of volcanoes, like the Cascades.

Tall and steep, ice-covered Mount Rainier is a particularly dangerous volcano. During previous eruptions its ice and snow melted instantly, creating mudflows—avalanches of mud and debris. The mudflows surged down the flanks of the mountain, burying the neighboring countryside in a thick layer of rubble. Mudflows on Rainier have extended as far as Puget Sound, destroying everything in their paths. Mount Rainer poses a greater threat than Mount St. Helens because it is much larger and threatens a more populated area. Its last major eruption was about 2,000 years ago.

The same plate movements that create an earthquake-and-volcano threat for Puget Sound also produce a tsunami hazard. A sudden shifting of the plates could launch a tsunami that could hit Washington and Oregon within minutes, and the California coast not long afterward.

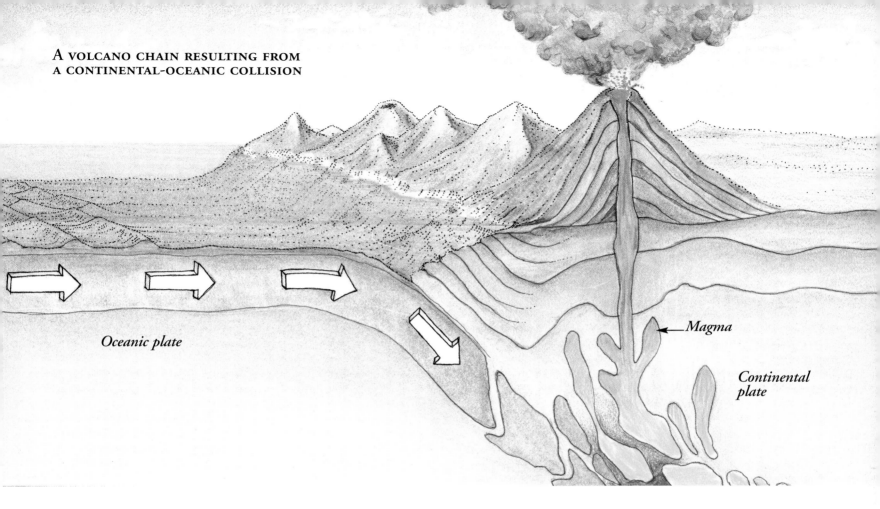

A VOLCANO CHAIN RESULTING FROM A CONTINENTAL-OCEANIC COLLISION

Oceanic plate

Magma

Continental plate

Oceanic-Oceanic Collisions. In a contest between two plates carrying oceanic crust, gravity drags the denser, older plate beneath the less dense, younger plate. What happens next is similar to a continental-oceanic collision. A trench forms and the denser plate is subducted. The "sweat" from the heated sinking plate rises and partially melts the overriding plate. However this time the magma burns through the overriding plate like a blowtorch. Punching through the ocean floor, it gives rise to a string of underwater volcanoes.

Over time the volcanoes may poke through the ocean surface, forming a curved chain of islands called an island arc. The arc's curve parallels the curved shape of the deep-sea trench. Japan, Indonesia, and the Aleutian Islands are island arcs.

Continental-Continental Collisions.

When two continents crash they buckle the crust, raising it into majestic mountains. Subduction plays no role here. Similar in density, neither land-bearing plate can ride over the other. The collision that produced the Himalayan Mountains began 50 million years ago when the plate that carries India bulldozed into Eurasia. The collision continues to this day, thrusting the Himalayas even higher.

If you peered down at a continent from space, the land would appear to be one solid mass. In reality each continent resembles a patchwork quilt with many different pieces. Over the eons, collisions between plates plastered volcanic islands together. Some of the fused islands grew into mini-continents.

More than a billion years ago, seven mini-continents melded to form the core of the North American continent. Since then bits and pieces of other islands and mini-continents have crashed into North America, increasing its size. Most of the land west of the Rocky Mountains, east of the Appalachian Mountains, and south of the Rio Grande was cemented on in this manner.

Continent-crunching forces built the Himalayan Mountains.

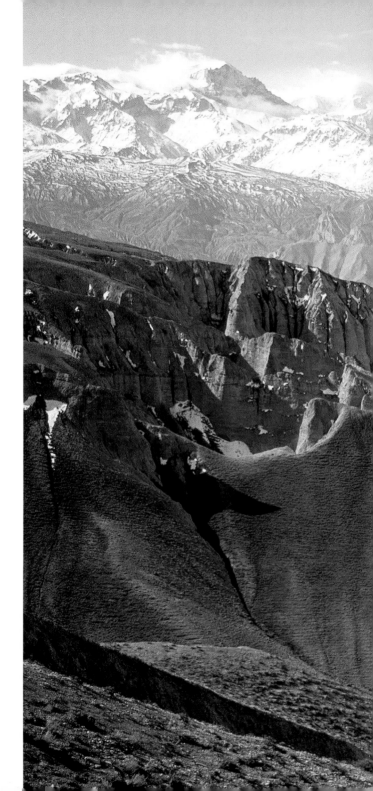

You may have learned that Europe and Asia are distinct continents. Yet if you look at a map, they appear to be one large body of land. Very long ago they were separate. But more than 300 million years ago they plowed into each other and merged into one large landmass. The Ural Mountains, the scar left over from their pileup, marks their ancient boundaries. Most science textbooks now refer to Asia and Europe as a single landmass, Eurasia.

PLATES THAT SCRAPE PAST EACH OTHER (TRANSFORM BOUNDARIES)

Transform boundaries occur where two plates squeeze sideways past each other, lumbering in opposite directions. The best-known transform boundary is California's San Andreas Fault. Here the North American plate, which totes practically all of North America, and the Pacific plate, which carts the Pacific Ocean floor and a thin slice of California, grind past one another. In most places, the rough edges of the plates jam, preventing movement. Stress builds up until the fault suddenly snaps and the plates jerk past each other, setting off an earthquake.

This mosque in Sakarya, Turkey, collapsed in 1999 during a 7.4-magnitude quake that killed at least 15,600 people. The quake occured along the Anatolian Fault, a transform fault similiar in length and destructive potential to the San Andreas Fault.

37

SEPARATING PLATES (DIVERGENT BOUNDARIES)

Divergent Boundaries in Water. Divergent boundaries arise where two plates pull away from each other. Here volcanoes sprout. Most divergent boundaries are found in the mid-ocean ridge, the longest mountain chain in the world. Concealed far beneath the Earth's oceans for most of its 40,000-mile (65,000-kilometer) length, the mid-ocean ridge loops around the planet like the stitching on a baseball. A valley a few hundred yards deep splits most sections of the ridge. Down the middle of the valley runs a crack in the ocean floor, the boundary between the plates.

Molten rock from the mantle spurts up through the crack and ultimately breaks through the surface in a volcanic eruption. The molten rock spreads out and hardens, temporarily welding the plates together. More molten rock gushes up from the crack. It splits the recently hardened rock and elbows it aside. This process, called seafloor spreading, continually creates new ocean floor and pushes it out along both sides of the ridge.

As oceanic crust moves away from the mid-ocean ridge, it cools, shrinks, and becomes denser. This cooling process takes millions of years. As the plates become more dense, they sink lower into the underlying asthenosphere. Consequently the older parts of the ocean floor lie at a greater depth than the younger parts.

Divergent Boundaries on Land. When a divergent boundary develops on land, the separating plates may rip apart a continent and give birth to a new ocean. The process begins when continental crust is lifted and stretched thin by molten rock flowing up from the mantle. Like an over-stretched rubber band, the weakened crust breaks easily. It slides apart, creating a deep valley called a rift.

As the rift widens, the valley floor sinks. Eventually the bottom may dip low enough for the ocean to rush in and fill the enlarging valley. The flooded valley becomes the basin of a young and growing ocean.

The Rio Grande rift in the western United States is a 6-mile-deep (10-kilometer) crack in the North American continent running from Colorado to Texas. It is concealed by a thick blanket of sediments and hardened lava. The course of the Rio Grande River traces the center of the rift's path. If the rift continues to expand, it may someday split the western United States away from the rest of the continent. If

Soaring above the surface of the North Atlantic Ocean, the mid-ocean ridge forms the island of Iceland. This Icelandic volcano is known as Lakagigar.

you live along the Rio Grande River, your home may be ocean-front property in 50 million years!

The ocean floor is recycled every 200 million years or so—the time needed for new ocean floor to emerge at the mid-ocean ridge, drift across the ocean, and disappear into a trench. If more of a plate is consumed in trenches than is created at the mid-ocean ridge, the plate will shrink. The Pacific Ocean, which is encircled by many trenches, is growing smaller. The Atlantic Ocean, with few trenches, is expanding.

HOT SPOTS

The birth announcement won't be needed for another 50,000 years, but the newest Hawaiian island is in the process of being born. Loihi, the youngest volcano in the Hawaiian chain, lies hidden about half a mile (.8 kilometer) beneath the waves about 20 miles (32 kilometers) south-east of the Big Island of Hawaii. Loihi soars more than 11,500 feet (3,500 meters) above the ocean floor. Someday its fiery peak may pile lava high enough to burst through the surface and become an island.

In 1996 swarms of earthquakes linked to magma movement within Loihi created a flurry of landslides on the volcano's steep slopes. The peak collapsed slowly, leaving a large crater. A rapid collapse could have spawned a huge tsunami. Future landslides may result in tsunamis power-ful enough to raze parts of the Big Island, as well as more distant sites such as the city of Honolulu on the island of Oahu.

Landslide debris litters the seabed surrounding all the Hawaiian Islands, evidence that giant rock chunks can peel off the sides of volcanoes. Sea cliffs on the islands bear scars from prehistoric tsunamis generated by such debris flows. Some scars show that one wave rose nearly 1,200 feet (366 meters) above sea level. This is about as high as the Empire State Building.

Landslides are part of the "growing pains" of volcanic islands. As a volcano increases in size, large chunks break off and tumble to the seafloor. A new peak may rise on the ruins of the old.

Loihi and her sisters, Kilauea and Mauna Loa, are among the world's

Lava spews from the Puu Oo crater on the eastern flank of Kilauea volcano. The current eruption of Kilauea started in January 1983. At the time this book was published in 2003, it showed no signs of decline.

most active volcanoes. They sit in the middle of the Pacific Ocean, far from any plate boundaries. These volcanoes are not a by-product of subduction like the volcanoes of island arcs. They owe their existence to a hot spot, which feeds them magma.

Geologists are still puzzling over the origin of hot spots. According to one theory, the hot spots are isolated pockets of magma. The magma comes from the top layer of the mantle and seeps up through thin spots in the rocky crust like a waterfall in reverse. Where the magma burbles up to the surface, volcanoes form.

However the most accepted theory contends that a hot spot originates in the deepest part of the mantle. It begins as a rising plume of extremely hot rock shaped like a balloon on a string. When the hot rock reaches the lithosphere, it melts the overlying plate and collects in a large pool. Just as a large pimple swells the overlying skin, the hot spot creates a bulge in the plate above it. A volcano appears when the hot rock pops completely through the plate. A single hot spot can power several different volcanoes, each with its own plumbing.

The Pacific plate drifts over the Hawaiian hot spot at a rate of 3 1/2 inches (9 centimeters) a year, dragging the plumbing along with it. The hot spot may be as wide as 200 miles (320 kilometers). Because the hot spot is so large, and the plate moves so slowly over it, a Hawaiian volcano may be active for at least two million years. However the plate movement finally severs the link between an active volcano and its magma source. The volcano dies, but a new one arises over the hot spot.

This process formed the Hawaiian Islands and has left a string of extinct volcanoes stretching from Hawaii to the Aleutian trench near Alaska. The ages of the islands increase with distance from the hot spot.

Younger islands show relatively few signs of erosion. But older ones crumble under the wearing forces of wind, rain, and waves. Some are worn nearly flat. Eventually all sink beneath the sea as the plate lugs them away from the elevated hot spot. Volcanoes are called seamounts when they do not protrude above the surface. Flat-topped seamounts are referred to as guyots.

At Puu Oo crater, brief periods of fountaining, where lava shoots 1,000 feet (300 m) into the air, alternate with much longer intervals of quieter activity.

THE OCEAN BASIN

The world ocean sits in the ultimate bathtub—a colossal basin edged by the continents. The ocean completely fills the basin. The overflow pours onto shallow land surrounding the continents.

The ocean-covered rim of a continent is called the continental margin. It extends from the coastline to the deep-sea floor. A continental margin is divided into three zones—the continental shelf, continental slope, and continental rise.

The continental shelf slants gently away from the coastline, jutting out an average of 40 miles (64 kilometers). It ends abruptly at a sharp cliff. The face of the cliff is the continental slope. The slope drops steeply from the continental shelf to the flat abyssal plain on the deep-ocean bottom. Sediments accumulating at the base of the slope form the continental rise.

The continental margin is extremely narrow where subduction takes place and the ocean floor dives beneath the continent. The continental slope actually forms a wall of the subduction trench. Narrow continental margins, such as those ringing the Pacific Ocean, are quite prone to earthquakes, volcanoes, and tsunamis. In contrast wider continental margins, like those skirting the Atlantic Ocean, are much quieter.

Nevertheless the east coast of the United States faces a tsunami risk, although a much slighter one than the risk for the Pacific Rim. Three small subduction trenches exist in the Atlantic Ocean—two in the eastern Caribbean Sea and one east of the southern tip of South America. These trenches are less active than the ones in the Pacific, so the Atlantic experiences fewer tsunamis.

Occasionally earthquakes rattle the Atlantic coasts of the United States and Canada. The cause of these quakes is not well understood yet.

At the same time as new rock appears at the mid-ocean ridge, old rock disappears in trenches near the edge of some continents and island groups. The old rock is dragged into the mantle, where it melts and is recycled. Ocean basins may grow bigger or smaller, but the overall size of the Earth remains the same.

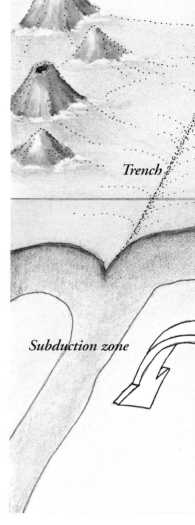

Trench

Subduction zone

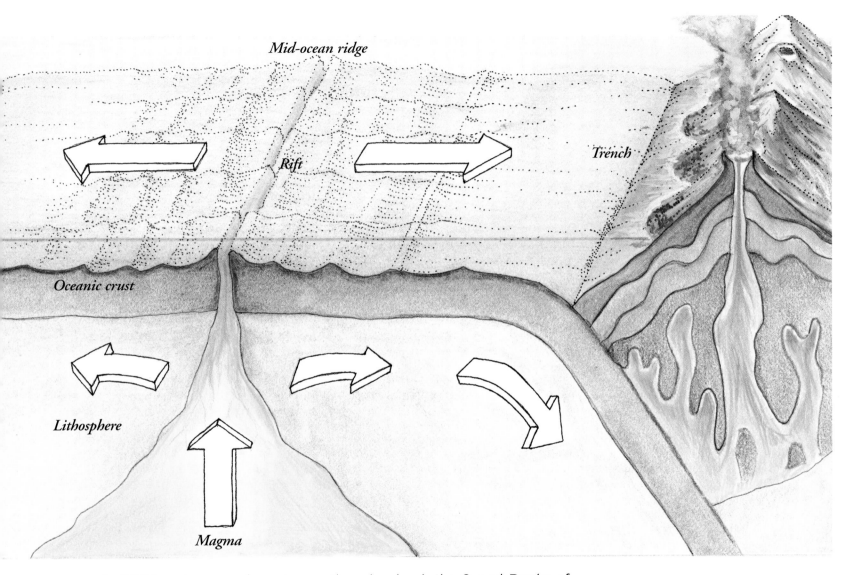

Mid-ocean ridge

Rift

Trench

Oceanic crust

Lithosphere

Magma

In 1929 a strong underwater earthquake shook the Grand Banks of Newfoundland, about 250 miles (400 kilometers) off the Canadian shore. It originated near the top of the continental slope and triggered a tsunami that took about 30 lives.

The quake also loosened mud and soggy sand on the continental shelf. The

45

loosened sediments rampaged down the continental slope in a catastrophic landslide known as a turbidity current. The current scoured out the sea floor beneath it and mixed the rubble into its flow. Traveling at a speed of about 40 miles (64 kilometers) per hour, the turbidity current severed 12 major transatlantic telegraph cables that lay in its path.

The cables stretched underwater from Newfoundland to Great Britain. They were used to send telegraph messages between Europe and North America. The cables closest to the earthquake's source snapped at the time of the quake. Other breaks, however, occurred along the sea floor as the turbidity current progressed down the continental slope. The last cable, which lay more than 500 miles (800 kilometers) from the continental shelf, was cut 13 hours after the initial shock. In all, the turbidity current traveled over 700 miles (1,127 kilometers) before losing momentum on the flat abyssal plain. It left a coating of mud 2 to 3 feet (60 to 90 centimeters) thick on the plain, covering more than 100,000 square miles (259,000 square kilometers).

Deep fissures riddle the steep continental slope off the coasts of New Jersey, Virginia, and North Carolina, setting the stage for similar turbidity currents. A large landslide could push enough water aside to pummel the neighboring shoreline with a tsunami 15 feet (4.6 meters) high. Fortunately the chance of this happening is quite small.

Giant Tsunami Threat in the Atlantic

Although tsunamis are rare in the Atlantic, an eruption of Cumbre Vieja volcano in the Canary Islands off West Africa could produce a monster wave. An eruption in 1949 produced a long crack on the side of the volcano. Future eruptions could deepen the crack, causing the flank to collapse and fall into the sea. The landslide would displace enough water to create a 325-foot (100-meter) wave along nearby African shores. Traveling at a speed up to 500 miles (800 kilometers) per hour, the tsunami would reach Florida within eight to nine hours. It would strike the coast with 160-foot-high (50-meter-high) waves and surge several miles inland. The entire eastern seaboard from Florida to Newfoundland, Canada, would be clobbered, including New York, Boston, and other major cities. Fortunately the volcano is not expected to erupt anytime soon.

Even the picturesque rocky coast of Maine is not immune to the risk of tsunamis.

The Slow Shuffle of Roving Plates

The planet-sculpting dance of the plates unfolds in ultra–slow motion. The slowest plate creeps along at a rate of less than 1/2 inch (1 centimeter) a year, while the speediest plate "gallops" ahead at 6 inches (15 centimeters) annually. Yet over millions of years, these small movements have brought about immense changes in the size, shape, and position of the Earth's lands and oceans.

Geologists are trying to reconstruct these changes. Using detective skills, they hunt for clues in the Earth's rocks. The farther back they search, the harder it is to piece together the story.

Nevertheless geologists have established the existence of a supercontinent called Rodina, which formed from the Earth's major landmasses about 1.1 billion years ago. The exact size and shape of Rodina is unknown. It broke up 750

More than 225 million years ago, Earth's major landmasses crunched together to form Pangaea, a supercontinent.

About 200 million years ago, rifting tore Pangaea into two parts. The split formed the southern continent, Gondwanaland, and the northern continent, Laurasia. It also gave birth to the budding Atlantic Ocean.

About 140 million years ago, additional rifts began to break up Gowanaland and Laurasia.

48

million years ago. About 150 million years later another supercontinent, Pannotia, was assembled from the pieces, but it was relatively short-lived, lasting only 50 million years or so.

Geologists believe that other supercontinents existed long before Rodina and Pannotia. The most recent supercontinent, Pangaea, appeared about 275 million years ago. The illustrations show how the positions of the continents have changed since then. Geologists predict that in 50 million years Australia will grind into southeast Asia. England will lie closer to the North Pole, and the western part of California and Mexico will be up the coast in British Columbia. If the present-day continents continue to drift at their current rate, in slightly more than 200 million years they will all bunch together again.

__About 60 million years ago,__ the Earth resembled it's present form, except that India was a separate continent on a collision course with Eurasia.

__The Earth today.__ India, which was previously attached to Antartica, has drifted 5,600 miles (9,000 km) in the past 200 million years—the greatest migration of any continent.

chapter 4

A TALE OF TWO CITIES:
ONE SUNKEN, ONE SINKING

A sunken city lies at the bottom of the Mediterranean Sea, about 4 miles (6.4 kilometers) off Egypt's north coast and 26 feet (8 meters) beneath the waves. Although in ruins, the submerged ghost town is amazingly complete. Preserved in the mushy sediments are relics of ancient buildings, sacred temples, giant pink statues, and remnants of canals and a once thriving harbor.

For more than a millennium the wreckage lay undisturbed beneath a thick layer of sediments. In 2000 a team of underwater archaeologists uncovered the ruins. The scientists identified the city as the long-lost seaport Herakleion, named for the Greek hero Hercules. One of the most valuable objects found in the ancient debris is a stela—an engraved black granite slab, 76 inches (195 centimeters) high. The engravings contained an edict from the reign of Pharaoh Nektanebos the First, who ruled Egypt from 378 to 362 B.C. It declares that Greek merchants had to pay a 10 percent tax on the goods they sold in the city. The taxes benefited the temple of Neith, the goddess of the hunt.

The archaeologists also uncovered the main temple of the supreme Egyptian god, Amon, and his son Khonsu, who was also known as Herakles. Inside the temple's thick walls lay three broken statues of a pharaoh, his queen, and Hapi, the Nile god of flooding. Pottery, utensils, a sphinx-shaped incense burner, gold jewelry, and gold and bronze coins were uncovered in this watery realm. Some coins found outside the temple walls date back to the eighth century A.D., proof that the city was still inhabited at that time.

Herakleion was once a bustling harbor town at the mouth of the Nile River. Egyptians built it when pharaohs still ruled. Resting on marshy land abutting the sea, the city thrived for more than a thousand years.

This ancient statue of the Egyptian god Hapi was one of many remarkable artifacts uncovered by divers in the sunken city of Herakleion.

Sometime during the eighth century A.D., Herakleion slipped into the sea. The subsidence, however, took place gradually over the span of a few centuries. The mystery of how Herakleion finally drowned has not been solved. But two theories exist. According to one, an earthquake tumbled Herakleion into its watery grave. Violent shaking could have turned the soft soil beneath the city into quicksand. As the ground became liquid ooze, the structures on it would have sunk. The columns of the temples all fell in one direction, a sign that an earthquake may have collapsed them. The Mediterranean is an earthquake-prone region.

According to the second theory, the Nile River was the culprit. The Nile is the world's longest river. From its beginnings in Uganda, the river winds about 4,000 miles (6,400 kilometers) through northeastern Africa. Above Cairo, Egypt, the Nile splits into several branches before spilling into the Mediterranean Sea. About 2,000 years ago, one of the main branches flowed past Herakleion.

The historical records show that the Nile experienced tremendous flooding in A.D. 741 and 742 The bloated river may have jumped its banks and soaked Herakleion. Waterlogged, the marshy land beneath the city could have turned to ooze, toppling the buildings and sinking the city. Another sunken city, Canopus, lies near Herakleion.

New Orleans and the Disappearing Mississippi Delta

Within your lifetime the United States may have its own sunken city— New Orleans, Louisiana. New Orleans is a southern port famous for its jazz bands, Cajun cooking, and annual Mardi Gras celebration. When French colonists established New Orleans alongside the Mississippi River in 1718, they built the settlement on a marshy ridge 3 feet (.9 meter) above sea level. Since then this festive city has been slowly sinking under its own weight. Today New Orleans lies an average of 6 1/2 feet (2 meters) below sea level.

The fate of New Orleans is tied to the Mississippi River. The Mississippi starts as a small stream that flows from Minnesota's Lake

The Nile Delta as seen from space.

Itasca. On its 2,340-mile (3,767-kilometer) trek to the Gulf of Mexico, the river gathers water from 31 states and 2 Canadian provinces. Along the way it also picks up silt, sand, mud, and other sediments.

When the Mississippi reaches the gulf, it slows and drops sediments. For millions of years, these sediments have gradually piled up. They have created a vast stretch of wetlands known as the Mississippi Delta. In the last 5,000 years, shifts in the river's flow have built up the modern delta first in one place then another, creating seven major lobes—distinct sections.

The delta is not stable. The sediments gradually press together, like a slice of fluffy bread flattened by a hand. As the sediments pack down, the land sinks. In the past, the Mississippi maintained its delta by depositing more sediments on top of the old.

The ground beneath New Orleans is part of the Mississippi Delta. Levees—large earthen walls—protect New Orleans from river flooding. Ironically this flood-control measure bears much of the blame for the city's sinking. The levees prevent the Mississippi from washing over and rebuilding the land with its muddy sediments. Over the years, the soil beneath New Orleans has packed down. This process continues today.

Fragile wetlands and barrier islands in the delta along Louisiana's coast buffer New Orleans from battering sea waves. When the city was first built, more than 100 miles (160 kilometers) of delta separated it from the Gulf of Mexico. But the wetlands and islands are rapidly disappearing. Between 1930 and 1990 the Louisiana coastline lost more than 1,000 square miles (2,590 square kilometers) of land. Now New Orleans lies just 50 miles (80 kilometers) or so from the sea.

Louisiana is losing between 25 and 35 square miles (65 to 91 square kilometers) of the delta a year. At this rate, there will be no natural barriers to prevent the ocean from reaching New Orleans by

Part of the delta along Louisiana's coast.

2050. New Orleans's end could come swiftly if storm-driven seas from a gargantuan hurricane overpower levees separating the city from the gulf and river.

The Mississippi Delta faces a constant threat from sinking land and erosion. But some of the loss is natural. Left on their own, rivers twist and turn. They sometimes shift course, changing where they drop their muddy deposits. Abandoned by a river, muck-starved wetlands sink and erode. This destruction is part of the natural life cycle of a delta.

Human interference, however, caused the bulk of the Mississippi Delta's woes. Construction of dams and levees throughout the Mississippi drainage system pinned the river and its major tributaries to fixed channels. These massive structures help to control floods and maintain shipping lanes.

But the dams trap sediments and dramatically reduce the amount of mud reaching the delta. The Mississippi, in its fixed channel, now sweeps much of its remaining sediments into the deep waters off the Gulf of Mexico. The sediments plunge down to the ocean floor or currents whisk them out to sea.

Making matters worse, the activities of the oil and gas industry in Louisiana have hastened the ruin of the Mississippi Delta. The United States depends on the oil and gas taken from Louisiana's coast. However canals dug for pipelines and access to drilling sites have destroyed precious wetlands. The canals have also permitted saltwater to move inland, killing freshwater plants vital to the delta's survival.

Another delta threat comes from nutrias, giant rodents that look like a cross between a beaver and a 30-pound (14-kilogram) rat. Native to South America, nutrias were brought to Louisiana in the 1930s to be bred and turned into fur coats. Some nutrias escaped from captivity and others were deliberately released into the wild. Millions of their descendants now make their homes in the wetlands along the Gulf of Mexico.

Nutrias devastate wetlands by gobbling up plant roots that bind together loose marshy soils. This leaves the soil open to erosion. To some extent, trappers used to control the nutria population by killing the pests for their pelts. However the demand for nutria fur dropped. So in 1998 officials from the United States Geological Survey, the National Wetlands Research Center, and

A nutria is a 2-foot-long (61-cm) rodent with fur similar to a beaver and a ratlike tail. If nutria meat appeals to enough appetites, this pest might be brought under control.

56

the Louisiana Department of Wildlife and Fisheries started a campaign called Save Our Wetlands—Eat Louisiana Nutria. They even sponsored a competition among some of Louisiana's top chefs for the best nutria recipes! They posted the winning recipes on the research center's Web site. The goal was to create a large demand for nutria meat so hunters would harvest the pests in large numbers.

Perhaps the delta's worst threat comes from rising sea levels. During the twentieth century, the sea level rose an average of 4 to 10 inches (10 to 25 centimeters) worldwide. Some scientists predict that it may climb 18 1/2 inches (47 centimeters) more by 2100 if the Earth warms by just an additional 4 degrees Fahrenheit (2.2 degrees Celsius). The Mississippi Delta can survive this calamity only if the wetlands build up faster and higher than the sea rises.

The impact of the delta's decline extends far beyond coastal Louisiana and the people who live and work there. About one-fifth of the nation's catch of fish and shellfish comes from the Gulf of Mexico. These marine animals spend part of their lives in the delta. For many, the wetlands serve as a breeding ground and nursery. A shrinking delta will mean fewer shrimps, crabs, oysters, and other seafood.

The marshy land provides a winter home for five million ducks and geese fleeing cold northern climates. If this habitat disappears, fewer waterfowl will survive and return to their summer homes in the northern United States and Canada. The delta also provides a rest stop for millions of birds that fly along the Mississippi during their fall and spring migrations. The disappearance of the delta and the nourishing food it provides will diminish these bird populations. The outlook for year-round wildlife—such as wading and shore birds, alligators, and muskrats—is not much better.

To slow the delta's destruction, Louisiana and federal agencies launched a plan in 1998 called Coast 2050. Its goal is to preserve the existing coastal wetlands and barrier islands. If Coast 2050 falls short, the sea will likely swallow the Louisiana coast. And New Orleans will become an underwater city like Herakleion.

Great egrets nest in the tree canopies in the Mississippi delta.

chapter 5

DOOMSDAY ROCKS

The world's greatest natural disasters were not triggered by volcanoes, earthquakes, or any other earthly phenomenon. Giant meteorites spawned them. Meteorites are asteroids or comets that reach the Earth and survive the fiery passage through the atmosphere to the planet surface.

About 35 million years ago, a meteorite about 2 to 3 miles (3 to 5 kilometers) across streaked into the Atlantic Ocean off the Virginia coast. The meteorite gouged out an immense crater 50 miles (81 kilometers) wide and more than a mile (1.6 kilometers) deep in the seafloor. The impact produced shock waves thousands of times stronger than any earthquake experienced in modern times. These shock waves raced out in all directions through the Earth's crust.

Winds carrying superheated rock blasted from the crater like a hurricane of fire. A tsunami of titanic proportions followed, pounding the shoreline with waves hundreds, or perhaps thousands, of feet high. Together the enormous tsunami waves and searing winds eradicated plants and animals as far away as present-day Boston, Massachusetts, and Charleston, South Carolina, leaving a barren wasteland.

Tsunami waves zoomed across the Atlantic and wreaked havoc along the coasts of Europe and Africa. However the meteorite impact produced no long-term global effects.

This is an artist's conception of an asteroid striking Earth.

The crater lies beneath Chesapeake Bay. Today an identical meteorite strike would kill tens of millions of people living along the eastern seaboard.

A larger meteorite struck with even deadlier consequences 65 million years ago, when dinosaurs populated the Earth. This doomsday rock was a flying mountain about 6 miles (10 kilometers) wide. With a blinding flash, it slammed into a shallow sea, covering what is now Mexico's Yucatán Peninsula. The collision sent shock waves through the planet and carved out a deep crater more than 100 miles (160 kilometers) wide in limestone and rock rich in sulfur. A second shock wave tore through the air. All living things within 60 miles (100 kilometers) of the impact died instantaneously.

A spectacular fireball of vaporized rock and rubble exploded through the atmosphere and out into space. A second fireball followed. As the superhot debris re-entered the atmosphere, the sky became an oven.

Broiling hot winds roared across the territories known today as Mexico and the United States. With the breath of fire, the winds roasted animals alive and transformed lush forests into oceans of flame. Within hours, mountains and valleys throughout North America turned into one huge blistered landscape. Firestorms raged on other continents, but the devastation was not as severe.

Meanwhile a tsunami at least 250 feet (75 meters) high crashed into Florida and the Gulf coast, swallowing the countryside and thrashing the continental margin, the ocean-covered rim of the continent. So great was the violence that mammoth submarine landslides were set in motion.

Dust from the fireballs and soot from the infernos permeated the atmosphere, blotting out the Sun. The darkness thrust the Earth into an "impact winter." Organisms worldwide that had survived the initial devastation now suffered. Without sufficient sunlight, plants died. And without enough plants, animals starved. Temperatures on the surface dipped 20 to 30 degrees Fahrenheit (11 to 17 degrees Celsius). The cold hastened the dying.

Perhaps an asteroid racing across the sky was the last image seen by many dinosaurs before they perished.

Among the hardest hit were the dinosaurs. Plant-eating dinosaurs perished from lack of food. Animal-eating dinosaurs died out when the plant eaters disappeared. The creatures that survived this mass extinction tended to be small, adaptable, widespread, and didn't require much food. Scavengers—animals that feasted on the remains of the dead—had an easier time than the others.

The impact had skyrocketed more than 100 billion tons of sulfur high into the atmosphere. The sulfur combined with water vapor to form tiny droplets of sulfuric acid. Nitric acid droplets were scattered throughout the atmosphere, too.

The nitric acid had formed when the intense heat in the atmosphere caused oxygen and nitrogen gas to combine. The new compound then joined with water vapor to form nitric acid. Over the next several months, most of the sulfuric-acid and nitric-acid droplets fell as acid rain. The acid poisoned the oceans, eating away the shells of marine organisms and disrupting ocean food chains.

Nearly all the debris in the cloud drifted to the surface of the Earth within half a year. But the impact had also flung immense quantities of limestone skyward, and this had even longer lasting consequences.

Limestone consists of carbon dioxide and calcium. The carbon dioxide escaped from the limestone and lingered in the atmosphere. Carbon dioxide is a greenhouse gas. Greenhouse gases trap heat energy. They become warmer as they absorb the heat. In turn, they warm the surrounding air and they also radiate some heat energy back toward the Earth's surface.

So the cold ended. But it was replaced with a period of global warming that probably lasted for thousands of years. Temperatures rose to sweltering levels, stressing the surviving organisms further. Almost two-thirds of the species living then disappeared forever.

The death of all the dinosaurs cleared the way for the rise of mammals, including human beings.

65

Comet Hale-Bopp over Mount Whitney. At its closest approach to Earth in spring 1997, Comet Hale-Bopp was still more than 100 million miles (31 million km) away.

At the same time that this planetwide die-off took place, a massive eruption of the Deccan Traps volcano in India was in full swing. In an eruption that lasted about 500,000 years, rivers of lava flowed from fissures—long cracks in the ground. The lava covered an area larger than all of California. The ash and carbon-dioxide gas released by the volcano may have played a major role in the prolonged global warming.

Other mass extinctions have occurred in the past when nearly all species of living things vanished. Interestingly nine of the ten greatest mass extinctions took place at a time when gargantuan fissure eruptions appeared. Some scientists believe that the impacts, fissure eruptions, and extinctions are linked. They think that the tremendous shock waves from an impact could jolt the planet hard enough to cause colossal outpourings of lava from the mantle. But the outpouring could happen only if a deep volcanic plume, like the one beneath the Big Island of Hawaii, already existed. The plume would provide a pathway for the mantle magma to reach the surface.

Death by Space Rocks

Comets and asteroids originated about 4.6 billion years ago from rubble left over from the creation of the Sun and planets. Asteroids are space rocks, ranging in size from dust particles to minimoons. Some contain metal; others do not. Most revolve around the Sun in the asteroid belt, a bagel-shaped ring between Mars and Jupiter. Some asteroids tumble in orbits that swing them close to the Earth. Occasionally the Earth's gravitational field snags an asteroid and drags it toward the planet. Small asteroids that burn up in the atmosphere are called meteors. Those that reach the surface are known as meteorites.

Comets that collide with the Earth are also known as meteorites. Comets are mountain-size clumps of frozen gases speckled throughout with space rock and dust. Most drift in orbits that lock them in the outer reaches of the solar system far past Pluto. Every so often an orbit whisks a comet dazzlingly close to the Earth and Sun. As the comet draws near the Sun, solar energy begins to vaporize the comet's volatile parts. (Volatile substances are solids or liquids that convert to gas easily.) Some of the ice changes to gas, making the head glow. Escaping gases and dust stretch out for millions of miles, forming the comet's tail.

Inset: On February 12, 1947, a meteorite made of iron fell near Novopoltavka, Siberia. When it entered the atmosphere, the meteorite broke into thousands of pieces, including this one, which weighs 4 pounds (1.8 kg).

Impacts with space debris in the Earth's infancy built up the planet from a speck of dust to its present size. Comets pelting the Earth after it reached full size contributed water vapor to the primitive atmosphere and ultimately the oceans. The heavy bombardment ended nearly 3.8 billion years ago. But stray rubble still zings the planet daily, most of it incinerating as it travels through the atmosphere.

The last large impact on Earth was a meteorite that exploded on June 30, 1908, over Tunguska, Siberia. Eyewitnesses in this sparsely settled region reported seeing a blinding-white fireball streak across the sky. The blast flattened and charred evergreen trees in an area about four times the size of New York City. It incinerated at least one large reindeer herd.

The fireball left no impact crater but the trees fell outward in a circular pattern beneath the center of the explosion. Scientists estimate that the meteorite's diameter was a scant 200 feet (61 meters). To cause a major disruption in the global climate, a celestial object must be at least 0.6 miles (1 kilometer) wide.

In 1994, images from the Hubble Space Telescope provided a glimpse of the destructive power of a comet in action. The images showed the comet Shoemaker-Levy approaching and striking the planet Jupiter. Jupiter's strong gravitational pull had ripped the comet into at least 20 large fragments. As the fragments hit the planet, plumes of fiery debris shot hundreds of miles above Jupiter. The impact of the fragments left dark red scars on Jupiter's surface that remained for months.

In 1908 a meteorite explosion over Tunguska, Siberia, destroyed more than 772 square miles (2,000 sq km) of forests, including the trees shown here.

SAFEGUARDING EARTH

Fortunately the chances of a giant impact happening in your lifetime are quite slim. Nevertheless scientists are exploring ways to defend the Earth against a doomsday comet or asteroid. They have ruled out blowing up a celestial threat with a nuclear bomb. The resulting fragments might still be large enough to inflict serious harm. Diverting the space rock away from Earth appears to be the safest solution. Here are some of the suggestions for altering the orbit of a cosmic object:

- Land a rocket on the comet or asteroid and use the push of the rocket's booster to launch the object into a safer path.
- Crash a rocket into the space rock to nudge it into a harmless orbit.
- Attach a huge solar sail to it and harness the solar wind like a sailboat harnesses the atmosphere's wind to change course. (Solar winds are streams of electrons and protons that escape from the Sun and travel away from the solar system at high speed.)
- Set off a nuclear bomb near the object to blast it off course.
- If the object is a comet, use lasers to boil off a portion of it. The resulting gases will propel the comet in a different direction.

CONCLUSION

While scientists may someday be able to prevent doomsday rocks from striking the Earth, they can't prevent tectonic plates from moving. The earthquakes, volcanoes, tsunamis, and changes in sea level caused by the shuffling of plates are inevitable and unstoppable. To reduce the death and destruction that may accompany them, scientists must expand their understanding of these events and learn to predict when and where they will occur.

Nuclear missiles could be used to change the course of an earthbound meteorite.

glossary

ABYSSAL PLAIN—a vast, flat region of the deep seafloor

ASTEROID—a space rock

ASTHENOSPHERE—a soft section of the Earth's mantle below the lithosphere

CALDERA—a huge pit on top of a volcano formed by the collapse of the volcanic cone

COMET—a clump of frozen gases that moves through space

CONTINENT—a vast landmass surrounded by the ocean

CONTINENTAL MARGIN—the water-covered area of a continent that extends from the shoreline to the deep-ocean floor

CONTINENTAL RISE—a thick accumulation of sediments on the deep-ocean floor that slid down the continental slope

CONTINENTAL SHELF—the shallow sea closest to the continent

CONTINENTAL SLOPE—the steep incline dropping down from the continental shelf to the continental rise of the ocean floor

CONVECTION—the movement of heat in a gas or liquid from a warm place to a cooler place

CONVECTION CURRENT—the movement within a fluid caused by density changes

CONVERGENT BOUNDARY—the border between two plates that are colliding with each other

CRUST—the hard outer layer of the earth

DELTA—the area at the mouth of a river that is built up from sediments

DENSITY—the amount of mass in a given volume

DIVERGENT BOUNDARY—the border between two plates that are moving away from each other

EARTHQUAKE—the shaking that results from ground movement along a fault

FAULT—a crack in the Earth's crust where rocks have moved past each other

FOCUS—the place where an earthquake originates

GLOBAL WARMING—a gradual increase in the average world temperature

HOT SPOT—a region where magma from the mantle melts through the overlying crust

Inner core—the innermost layer of the Earth

Lava—melted rock that flows out of a volcano

Liquification—the process by which water-soaked land turns to quicksand

Lithosphere—a rigid layer composed of the upper mantle and overlying crust

Magma—melted rock beneath the surface of the rock

Magnetic field—the area around a magnet in which its force affects objects

Mantle—an inner layer of the Earth located between the outer core and the crust

Meteorites—asteroids or comets that reach the Earth

Mid-ocean ridge—the undersea mountain chain

Moment-magnitude scale—a scale that rates earthquakes by calculating the total amount of energy they release

Mouth—the place where a river flows into the sea

Mudflow—a huge volume of water mixed with soil and volcanic rubble that travels rapidly down the slopes of a volcano

Nutrias—large rodents

Outer core—an inside layer of the earth sandwiched between the inner core and the mantle

Plate tectonics—a scientific theory that explains the cause of the Earth's volcanoes, earthquakes, and mountain ranges in terms of plate movements

Plates (See Tectonic plate)

Pyroclastic flows—avalanches of hot gas and debris that speed down a volcano's flanks

Rift valley—a deep valley formed by separating plates

Sea level—the height of the ocean

Seafloor spreading—the process by which new molten material is added to the ocean floor along the boundaries of spreading plates

Sediments—small solid particles that come from rocks or the remains of living things

Seismic wave—a vibration generated by an earthquake that travels through the Earth

Seismograph—an instrument that detects and records vibrations produced by an earthquake

Subduction—the process by which an oceanic plate sinks beneath another plate

Subsidence—the dropping of land from a higher elevation to a lower elevation

Tectonic plate—one of more than a dozen segments of the lithosphere that move independently

Transform boundary—the border between two plates that are moving sideways relative to each other

Tremblor—an earthquake

Trench—a deep canyon on the ocean floor

Tsunami—a large destructive wave caused by a landslide or earthquake on the ocean floor

Turbidity current—an underwater avalanche

Volcano—a place where magma emerges through a weak spot in the Earth's crust

Wave—the movement of energy through water

Wetlands—marshes, bogs, and swamps

further reading

BOOKS

Downs, Sandra. Earth's Fiery Fury. Brookfield, CT: Twenty-First Century Books, 2000.

Gallant, Roy A. Dance of the Continents. Tarrytown, NY: Marshall Cavendish, 2000.

Lambert, David. The Kingfisher Young People's Book of Oceans. New York: Kingfisher, 1997.

Lauber, Patricia. Flood: Wrestling with the Mississippi. Washington, D.C.: National Geographic Society, 1996.

Patent, Dorothy Hinshaw, with photographs by William Munoz. Shaping the Earth. New York: Clarion Books, 2000.

Sattler, Helen Roney, with illustrations by Giulio Maestro. Our Patchwork Planet. New York: Lothrop, Lee & Shepard Books, 1995.

Vogel, Carole G. Nature's Fury: Eyewitness Reports of Natural Disasters. New York: Scholastic, 2000.

WEB SITES

"Aboukir 2001: Sunken Herakleion—Between Reality and Legends." A Web site sponsored by Franck Giddio, who headed the underwater expedition that discovered the sunken city of Herakleion.

http://www.franckgiddio.org/english/projects/aboukir/default.asp

BusinessWeek Online: "Come 2100, New Orleans Could Be an Underwater Attraction" by Alan Hall

http://www.businessweek.com/bwdaily/dnflash/feb2000/nf00201f.htm

California Academy of Sciences: "The Next Wave" by Anne M. Rosenthal published on-line in California Wild (Spring 1999). Describes the Papua New Guinea disaster and other tsunamis.

CWPPRA: Louisiana Coastal Restoration Web Site: "The Cost of Doing Nothing"

http://www.lacoast.gov/Programs/CWPPRA/Watermarks/summer99/thecost.htm

NASA: "Tsunami, The Big Wave"

http://observe.ivv.nasa.gov/nasa/exhibits/tsunami/tsun_bay.html

Southern California Earthquake Center: "A Comparison of the February 28, 2001, Nisqually, Washington, and January 17, 1994, Northridge, California, Earthquakes"

http://www.scec.org/instanet/01news/feature010313.html

U.S. Geological Survey and the National Park Service's Web Site: "What on Earth Is Plate Tectonics?"

http://wrgis.wr.usgs.gov/docs/parks/pltec/pltec1.html

University of Alaska Sea Grant College Program: "The Next Big Earthquake in Alaska May Come Sooner Than You Think." Provides earthquake safety dos and don'ts, information on reducing earthquake damage, and earthquake and tsunami facts.

http://www.uaf.edu/seagrant/earthquake/index.html

selected bibliography

BOOKS

Alverez, Walter. T. Rex and the Crater of Doom. Princeton, NJ: Princeton University Press, 1997.

Decker, Robert W., and Barbara B. Decker. Mountains of Fire: The Nature of Volcanoes. Cambridge, England: Cambridge University Press, 1991.

Dudley, Walter C., and Min Lee. Tsunami! 2d. ed. Honolulu: University of Hawaii Press, 1998.

Duxbury, Alyn C., Alison B. Duxbury, and Keith A. Sverdrup. An Introduction to the World's Oceans, 6th ed. New York: McGraw Hill, 2000.

Gribbin, John and Mary. Fire on Earth: Doomsday, Dinosaurs, and Humankind. New York: St. Martin's Press, 1996.

Poag, C. Wylie. Chesapeake Invader: Discovering America's Giant Meteorite Crater. Princeton, NJ: Princeton University Press, 1999.

Prager, Ellen J. Furious Earth. New York: McGraw Hill, 2000.

Tarbuck, Edward J., and Frederick K. Lutgens. Earth Science, 9th ed. Upper Saddle River, NJ: Prentice Hall, 2000.

Vogel, Carole G. Prentice Hall Science Explorer: Inside Earth. Upper Saddle River, NJ: Prentice Hall, 2000.

Vogel, Shawna. Naked Earth: The New Geophysics. New York: Dutton, 1995.

Woodard, Colin. Ocean's End: Travels Through Endangered Seas. New York: Basic Books, 2000.

WEB SITES

Students in the Science Communications Graduate Studies Program at the University of California, Santa Cruz: Science Notes 1999, "Killer Surf" by Krista Conger, illustrated by Zeke Smith

http://scicom.ucsc.edu/SciNotes/9901/kill/kill.htm

West Coast & Alaska Tsunami Warning Center, March 2, 2001: "Physics of Tsunamis"

http://wcatwc.gov/physics.htm

about the author

Award-winning author Carole Garbuny Vogel loves the ocean and lives 90 minutes from the beach. Her favorite water sport is boogie boarding, which is a lot like surfing but instead of standing up on the board, she lies flat. On beach days when the waves are small, Carole enjoys reading a good book or strolling on the sand looking for shells.

On workdays, Carole Vogel can usually be found "chained" to her computer, wrestling with words. She specializes in high-interest nonfiction topics for young people. Among her many books are *Nature's Fury: Eyewitness Reports of Natural Disasters* (winner of the Boston Authors Club Book of the Year Award), *Legends of Landforms: Native American Lore and the Geology of the Land* (an NCSS/CBC Notable Social Studies Trade Book), and *Shock Waves Through Los Angeles: The Northridge Earthquake* (placed on the Children's Literature Choice List). Carole Vogel is the coauthor of *The Great Yellowstone Fire*, which was named one of the 100 Best Children's Books of the Century by *The Boston Parents' Paper*.

Carole Vogel's books have been chosen for many reading lists, including Outstanding Science Trade Books by the NSTA-CBC, Best Children's Books of the Year by the Children's Book Committee at Bank Street College of Education, and the Science Books & Films' Best Books for Junior High and High School.

A native Pennsylvanian, Carole Vogel grew up in Pittsburgh and graduated from Kenyon College in Gambier, Ohio, with a B.A. in biology. She received an M.A.T. in elementary education from the University of Pittsburgh and taught for five years before becoming a science editor and author. She keeps in touch with her readership by giving author presentations in schools and libraries.

Carole and her husband, Mark, live in Lexington, Massachusetts, where they enjoy frequent visits from their two children, who recently graduated from college. You can learn more about Carole Vogel at her Web site: *http://www.recognitionscience.com/cgv/*